THE WESTMINSTER
SHORTER CATECHISM

THE WESTMINSTER SHORTER CATECHISM

With Scripture Proofs

THE BANNER OF TRUTH TRUST

THE BANNER OF TRUTH TRUST

Head Office
3 Murrayfield Road
Edinburgh, EH12 6EL
UK

North America Office
610 Alexander Spring Rd.
Carlisle, PA 17015
USA

banneroftruth.org

© The Banner of Truth Trust 2008
Reprinted 2010, 2012
Retypeset 2018
Reprinted 2021
Reprinted 2023

*

ISBN 978 0 85151 265 5

*

Typeset in 10/12 pt Adobe Garamond Pro
at The Banner of Truth Trust, Edinburgh

Printed in the USA by
Versa Press, Inc.,
EastPeoria, IL

Inside cover picture: The Westminster Assembly in session,
from a painting by John Rogers Herbert (1810-90)

THE SHORTER CATECHISM
With Scripture Proofs

Q. 1. What is the chief end of man?

A. Man's chief end is to glorify God,[1] and to enjoy him forever.[2]

[1] *1 Cor.* 10:31: Whether therefore ye eat, or drink, or whatsoever ye do, do all to the glory of God.

[2] *Psa.* 73:25-26: Whom have I in heaven but thee? and there is none upon earth that I desire beside thee. 26 My flesh and my heart faileth: but God is the strength of my heart, and my portion for ever.

Q. 2. What rule hath God given to direct us how we may glorify and enjoy him?

A. The Word of God, which is contained in the Scriptures of the Old and New Testaments,[1] is the only rule to direct us how we may glorify and enjoy him.[2]

[1] *Eph.* 2:20: And are built upon the foundation of the apostles and prophets, Jesus Christ himself being the chief corner stone. 2 *Tim.* 3:16: All scripture is given by inspiration of God, and is profitable for doctrine, for reproof, for correction, for instruction in righteousness.

[2] *1 John* 1:3: That which we have seen and heard declare we unto you, that ye also may have fellowship with us: and truly our fellowship is with the Father, and with his Son Jesus Christ.

Q. 3. What do the Scriptures principally teach?

A. The Scriptures principally teach what man is to believe concerning God, and what duty God requires of man.[1]

[1] *2 Tim.* 1:13: Hold fast the form of sound words, which thou hast heard of me, in faith and love which is in Christ Jesus.

Q. 4. What is God?

A. God is a Spirit,[1] infinite,[2] eternal,[3] and unchangeable,[4] in his being,[5] wisdom,[6] power,[7] holiness,[8] justice, goodness, and truth.[9]

[1] *John* 4:24: God is a Spirit: and they that worship him must worship him in spirit and in truth.

[2] *Job* 11:7: Canst thou by searching find out God? canst thou find out the Almighty unto perfection?

[3] *Psa.* 90:2: Before the mountains were brought forth, or ever thou hadst formed the earth and the world, even from everlasting to everlasting, thou art God.

[4] *James* 1:17: Every good gift and every perfect gift is from above, and cometh down from the Father of lights, with whom is no variableness, neither shadow of turning.

[5] *Exod.* 3:14: And God said unto Moses, I AM THAT I AM: and he said, Thus shalt thou say unto the children of Israel, I AM hath sent me unto you.

[6] *Psa.* 147:5: Great is our Lord, and of great power: his understanding is infinite.

[7] *Rev.* 4:8: Holy, holy, holy, Lord God Almighty, which was, and is, and is to come.

[8] *Rev.* 15:4: Who shall not fear thee, O Lord, and glorify thy name? for thou only art holy.

[9] *Exod.* 34:6-7: And the LORD passed by before him, and proclaimed, The LORD, The LORD God, merciful and gracious, longsuffering, and abundant in goodness and truth, [7] keeping mercy for thousands, forgiving iniquity and transgression and sin, and that will by no means clear the guilty.

Q. 5. Are there more Gods than one?

A. There is but one only,[1] the living and true God.[2]

[1] *Deut.* 6:4: Hear, O Israel: The LORD our God is one LORD.

[2] *Jer.* 10:10: But the LORD is the true God, he is the living God, and an everlasting king.

Q. 6. How many persons are there in the Godhead?

A. There are three persons in the Godhead: the Father, the Son, and the Holy Ghost;[1] and these three are one God, the same in substance, equal in power and glory.[2]

[1] *Matt.* 28:19: Go ye therefore, and teach all nations, baptizing them in the name of the Father, and of the Son, and of the Holy Ghost.
[2] 1 *John* 5:7: For there are three that bear record in heaven, the Father, the Word, and the Holy Ghost: and these three are one.

Q. 7. What are the decrees of God?

A. The decrees of God are, his eternal purpose, according to the counsel of his will, whereby, for his own glory, he hath foreordained whatsoever comes to pass.[1]

[1] *Eph.* 1:11-12: In whom also we have obtained an inheritance, being predestinated according to the purpose of him who worketh all things after the counsel of his own will: [12] that we should be to the praise of his glory.

Q. 8. How doth God execute his decrees?

A. God executeth his decrees in the works of creation[1] and providence.[2]

[1] *Rev.* 4:11: Thou hast created all things, and for thy pleasure they are and were created.
[2] *Dan.* 4:35: He doeth according to his will in the army of heaven, and among the inhabitants of the earth.

Q. 9. What is the work of creation?

A. The work of creation is, God's making all things of

nothing,[1] by the word of his power,[2] in the space of six days, and all very good.[3]

[1] *Gen.* 1:1: In the beginning God created the heaven and the earth.

[2] *Heb.* 11:3: Through faith we understand that the worlds were framed by the word of God, so that things which are seen were not made of things which do appear.

[3] *Gen.* 1:31: And God saw every thing that he had made, and, behold, it was very good.

Q. 10. How did God create man?

A. God created man male and female, after his own image,[1] in knowledge, righteousness, and holiness,[2] with dominion over the creatures.[3]

[1] *Gen.* 1:27: So God created man in his own image, in the image of God created he him; male and female created he them.

[2] *Col.* 3:10: And have put on the new man, which is renewed in knowledge after the image of him that created him. *Eph.* 4:24: And that ye put on the new man, which after God is created in righteousness and true holiness.

[3] *Gen.* 1:28: And God blessed them, and God said unto them, Be fruitful, and multiply, and replenish the earth, and subdue it: and have dominion over the fish of the sea, and over the fowl of the air, and over every living thing that moveth upon the earth.

Q. 11. What are God's works of providence?

A. God's works of providence are, his most holy,[1] wise,[2] and powerful preserving[3] and governing all his creatures, and all their actions.[4]

[1] *Psa.* 145:17: The LORD is righteous in all his ways, and holy in all his works.

[2] *Isa.* 28:29: This also cometh forth from the LORD of hosts, which is wonderful in counsel, and excellent in working.

[3] *Heb.* 1:3: Upholding all things by the word of his power.

⁴ *Psa.* 103:19: The LORD hath prepared his throne in the heavens; and his kingdom ruleth over all. *Matt.* 10:29: Are not two sparrows sold for a farthing? and one of them shall not fall on the ground without your Father.

Q. 12. What special act of providence did God exercise toward man in the estate wherein he was created?

A. When God had created man, he entered into a covenant of life with him, upon condition of perfect obedience;[1] forbidding him to eat of the tree of the knowledge of good and evil, upon the pain of death.[2]

[1] *Gal.* 3:12: And the law is not of faith: but, The man that doeth them shall live in them.
[2] *Gen.* 2:17: But of the tree of the knowledge of good and evil, thou shalt not eat of it: for in the day that thou eatest thereof thou shalt surely die.

Q. 13. Did our first parents continue in the estate wherein they were created?

A. Our first parents, being left to the freedom of their own will, fell from the estate wherein they were created, by sinning against God.[1]

[1] *Eccles.* 7:29: God hath made man upright; but they have sought out many inventions.

Q. 14. What is sin?

A. Sin is any want of conformity unto, or transgression of, the law of God.[1]

[1] 1 *John* 3:4: Whosoever committeth sin transgresseth also the law: for sin is the transgression of the law.

Q. 15. What was the sin whereby our first parents fell from the estate wherein they were created?

A. The sin whereby our first parents fell from the estate wherein they were created, was their eating the forbidden fruit.[1]

[1] *Gen.* 3:6-8: And when the woman saw that the tree was good for food, and that it was pleasant to the eyes, and a tree to be desired to make one wise, she took of the fruit thereof, and did eat, and gave also unto her husband with her; and he did eat. [7] And the eyes of them both were opened, and they knew that they were naked; and they sewed fig leaves together, and made themselves aprons. [8] And they heard the voice of the LORD God walking in the garden in the cool of the day: and Adam and his wife hid themselves from the presence of the LORD God amongst the trees of the garden.

Q. 16. Did all mankind fall in Adam's first transgression?

A. The covenant being made with Adam, not only for himself, but for his posterity;[1] all mankind, descending from him by ordinary generation, sinned in him, and fell with him, in his first transgression.[2]

[1] *Gen.* 1:28: And God blessed them, and God said unto them, Be fruitful, and multiply, and replenish the earth. *Gen.* 2:16-17: And the LORD God commanded the man, saying, Of every tree of the garden thou mayest freely eat: [17] But of the tree of the knowledge of good and evil, thou shalt not eat of it: for in the day that thou eatest thereof thou shalt surely die.
[2] *Rom.* 5:18: By the offence of one judgment came upon all men to condemnation.

Q. 17. Into what estate did the fall bring mankind?

A. The fall brought mankind into an estate of sin and misery.[1]

[1] *Rom.* 5:12: By one man sin entered into the world, and death by sin; and so death passed upon all men, for that all have sinned.

Q. 18. Wherein consists the sinfulness of that estate whereinto man fell?

A. The sinfulness of that estate whereinto man fell, consists in the guilt of Adam's first sin,[1] the want of original righteousness,[2] and the corruption of his whole nature, which is commonly called Original Sin;[3] together with all actual transgressions which proceed from it.[4]

[1] *Rom.* 5:19: By one man's disobedience many were made sinners.
[2] *Rom.* 3:10: There is none righteous, no, not one.
[3] *Eph.* 2:1: You hath he quickened, who were dead in trespasses and sins. *Psa.* 51:5: Behold, I was shapen in iniquity; and in sin did my mother conceive me.
[4] *Matt.* 15:19-20: For out of the heart proceed evil thoughts, murders, adulteries, fornications, thefts, false witness, blasphemies: [20] These are the things which defile a man.

Q. 19. What is the misery of that estate whereinto man fell?

A. All mankind by their fall lost communion with God,[1] are under his wrath and curse,[2] and so made liable to all the miseries of this life, to death itself, and to the pains of hell forever.[2]

[1] *Gen.* 3:8, 24: And they heard the voice of the LORD God walking in the garden in the cool of the day: and Adam and his wife hid themselves from the presence of the LORD God amongst the trees of the garden. [24] So he drove out the man.
[2] *Eph.* 2:3: And were by nature the children of wrath, even as others.

Gal. 3:10: Cursed is every one that continueth not in all things which are written in the book of the law to do them.

³ *Rom.* 6:23: The wages of sin is death. *Matt.* 25:41: Then shall he say also unto them on the left hand, Depart from me, ye cursed, into everlasting fire, prepared for the devil and his angels.

Q. 20. Did God leave all mankind to perish in the estate of sin and misery?

A. God having, out of his mere good pleasure, from all eternity, elected some to everlasting life,¹ did enter into a covenant of grace to deliver them out of the estate of sin and misery, and to bring them into an estate of salvation by a Redeemer.²

¹ *Eph.* 1:4: According as he hath chosen us in him before the foundation of the world.

² *Rom.* 3:21-22: But now the righteousness of God without the law is manifested, being witnessed by the law and the prophets; ²² Even the righteousness of God which is by faith of Jesus Christ unto all and upon all them that believe.

Q. 21. Who is the Redeemer of God's elect?

A. The only Redeemer of God's elect is the Lord Jesus Christ,¹ who, being the eternal Son of God, became man,² and so was, and continueth to be, God and man in two distinct natures, and one person,³ forever.⁴

¹ 1 *Tim.* 2:5: For there is one God, and one mediator between God and men, the man Christ Jesus.

² *John* 1:14: And the Word was made flesh, and dwelt among us.

³ *Rom.* 9:5: Whose are the fathers, and of whom as concerning the flesh Christ came, who is over all, God blessed for ever. Amen.

⁴ *Heb.* 7:24: But this man, because he continueth ever, hath an unchangeable priesthood.

Q. 22. How did Christ, being the Son of God, become man?

A. Christ, the Son of God, became man, by taking to himself a true body,[1] and a reasonable soul,[2] being conceived by the power of the Holy Ghost, in the womb of the Virgin Mary, and born of her,[3] yet without sin.[4]

[1] *Heb.* 2:14: Forasmuch then as the children are partakers of flesh and blood, he also himself likewise took part of the same.

[2] *Matt.* 26:38: Then saith he unto them, My soul is exceeding sorrowful, even unto death.

[3] *Luke* 1:31, 35: And, behold, thou shalt conceive in thy womb, and bring forth a son, and shalt call his name JESUS. 35 And the angel answered and said unto her, The Holy Ghost shall come upon thee, and the power of the Highest shall overshadow thee: therefore also that holy thing which shall be born of thee shall be called the Son of God.

[4] *Heb.* 7:26: Such an high priest became us, who is holy, harmless, undefiled, separate from sinners.

Q. 23. What offices doth Christ execute as our Redeemer?

A. Christ, as our Redeemer, executeth the offices of a prophet,[1] of a priest,[2] and of a king,[3] both in his estate of humiliation and exaltation.

[1] *Acts* 3:22: Moses truly said unto the fathers, A prophet shall the Lord your God raise up unto you of your brethren, like unto me; him shall ye hear in all things whatsoever he shall say unto you.

[2] *Heb.* 5:6: As he saith also in another place, Thou art a priest for ever after the order of Melchisedec.

[3] *Psa.* 2:6: Yet have I set my king upon my holy hill of Zion.

Q. 24. How doth Christ execute the office of a prophet?

A. Christ executeth the office of a prophet, in revealing

to us,[1] by his Word[2] and Spirit,[3] the will of God for our salvation.

[1] *John* 1:18: No man hath seen God at any time; the only begotten Son, which is in the bosom of the Father, he hath declared him.
[2] *John* 20:31: But these are written, that ye might believe that Jesus is the Christ, the Son of God; and that believing ye might have life through his name.
[3] *John* 14:26: The Comforter, which is the Holy Ghost, whom the Father will send in my name, he shall teach you all things.

Q. 25. How doth Christ execute the office of a priest?

A. Christ executeth the office of a priest, in his once offering up of himself a sacrifice to satisfy divine justice,[1] and reconcile us to God,[2] and in making continual intercession for us.[3]

[1] *Heb.* 9:28: Christ was once offered to bear the sins of many.
[2] *Heb.* 2:17: In all things it behoved him to be made like unto his brethren, that he might be a merciful and faithful high priest in things pertaining to God, to make reconciliation for the sins of the people.
[3] *Heb.* 7:25: He is able also to save them to the uttermost that come unto God by him, seeing he ever liveth to make intercession for them.

Q. 26. How doth Christ execute the office of a king?

A. Christ executeth the office of a king, in subduing us to himself,[1] in ruling and defending us,[2] and in restraining and conquering all his and our enemies.[3]

[1] *Psa.* 110:3: Thy people shall be willing in the day of thy power.
[2] *Isa.* 33:22 For the LORD is our judge, the LORD is our lawgiver, the LORD is our king; he will save us.
[3] 1 *Cor.* 15:25: For he must reign, till he hath put all enemies under his feet.

[14]

Q. 27. Wherein did Christ's humiliation consist?

A. Christ's humiliation consisted in his being born, and that in a low condition,[1] made under the law,[2] undergoing the miseries of this life,[3] the wrath of God,[4] and the cursed death of the cross;[5] in being buried, and continuing under the power of death for a time.[6]

[1] *Luke* 2:7: And she brought forth her firstborn son, and wrapped him in swaddling clothes, and laid him in a manger.

[2] *Gal.* 4:4: But when the fulness of the time was come, God sent forth his Son, made of a woman, made under the law.

[3] *Isa.* 53:3: He is despised and rejected of men; a man of sorrows, and acquainted with grief.

[4] *Matt.* 27:46: And about the ninth hour Jesus cried with a loud voice, saying, My God, my God, why hast thou forsaken me?

[5] *Phil.* 2:8: He humbled himself, and became obedient unto death, even the death of the cross.

[6] *Matt.* 12:40: As Jonas was three days and three nights in the whale's belly; so shall the Son of man be three days and three nights in the heart of the earth.

Q. 28. Wherein consisteth Christ's exaltation?

A. Christ's exaltation consisteth in his rising again from the dead on the third day,[1] in ascending up into heaven, in sitting at the right hand of God the Father,[2] and in coming to judge the world at the last day.[3]

[1] 1 *Cor.* 15:4: And that he was buried, and that he rose again the third day according to the scriptures

[2] *Mark* 16:19: So then after the Lord had spoken unto them, he was received up into heaven, and sat on the right hand of God.

[3] *Acts* 17:31: He hath appointed a day, in the which he will judge the world in righteousness by that man whom he hath ordained; whereof he hath given assurance unto all men, in that he hath raised him from the dead.

Q. 29. How are we made partakers of the redemption purchased by Christ?

A. We are made partakers of the redemption purchased by Christ, by the effectual application of it to us[1] by his Holy Spirit.[2]

[1] *John* 1:12: But as many as received him, to them gave he power to become the sons of God, even to them that believe on his name.

[2] *Titus* 3:5-6: Not by works of righteousness which we have done, but according to his mercy he saved us, by the washing of regeneration, and renewing of the Holy Ghost; [6] Which he shed on us abundantly through Jesus Christ our Saviour.

Q. 30. How doth the Spirit apply to us the redemption purchased by Christ?

A. The Spirit applieth to us the redemption purchased by Christ, by working faith in us,[1] and thereby uniting us to Christ in our effectual calling.[2]

[1] *Eph.* 2:8: For by grace are ye saved through faith; and that not of yourselves: it is the gift of God.

[2] *Eph.* 3:17: That Christ may dwell in your hearts by faith &c. 1 *Cor.* 1:9: God is faithful, by whom ye were called unto the fellowship of his Son Jesus Christ.

Q. 31. What is effectual calling?

A. Effectual calling is the work of God's Spirit,[1] whereby, convincing us of our sin and misery,[2] enlightening our minds in the knowledge of Christ,[3] and renewing our wills,[4] he doth persuade and enable us to embrace Jesus Christ, freely offered to us in the gospel.[5]

[1] 2 *Tim.* 1:9: Who hath saved us, and called us with an holy calling.

[2] *Acts* 2:37: Now when they heard this, they were pricked in their heart, and said unto Peter and to the rest of the apostles, Men and brethren, what shall we do?

[3] *Acts* 26:18: To open their eyes, and to turn them from darkness to light, and from the power of Satan unto God.

[4] *Ezek.* 36:26: A new heart also will I give you, and a new spirit will I put within you: and I will take away the stony heart out of your flesh, and I will give you an heart of flesh.

[5] *John* 6:44-45: No man can come to me, except the Father which hath sent me draw him: and I will raise him up at the last day. [45] Every man therefore that hath heard, and hath learned of the Father, cometh unto me.

Q. 32. What benefits do they that are effectually called partake of in this life?

A. They that are effectually called do in this life partake of justification,[1] adoption,[2] and sanctification, and the several benefits which in this life do either accompany or flow from them.[3]

[1] *Rom.* 8:30: Moreover whom he did predestinate, them he also called: and whom he called, them he also justified: and whom he justified, them he also glorified.

[2] *Eph.* 1:5: Having predestinated us unto the adoption of children by Jesus Christ to himself.

[3] 1 *Cor.* 1:30: But of him are ye in Christ Jesus, who of God is made unto us wisdom, and righteousness, and sanctification, and redemption.

Q. 33. What is justification?

A. Justification is an act of God's free grace, wherein he pardoneth all our sins,[1] and accepteth us as righteous in his sight,[2] only for the righteousness of Christ imputed to us,[3] and received by faith alone.[4]

[1] *Eph.* 1:7: In whom we have redemption through his blood, the forgiveness of sins, according to the riches of his grace.

[2] 2 *Cor.* 5:21: For he hath made him to be sin for us, who knew no sin; that we might be made the righteousness of God in him.

[3] *Rom.* 5:19: For as by one man's disobedience many were made sinners, so by the obedience of one shall many be made righteous.

[4] *Gal.* 2:16: Knowing that a man is not justified by the works of the law, but by the faith of Jesus Christ.

Q. 34. What is adoption?

A. Adoption is an act of God's free grace,[1] whereby we are received into the number, and have a right to all the privileges of the sons of God.[2]

[1] 1 *John* 3:1: Behold, what manner of love the Father hath bestowed upon us, that we should be called the sons of God!

[2] *John* 1:12: As many as received him, to them gave he power to become the sons of God, even to them that believe on his name. *Rom.* 8:17: And if children, then heirs; heirs of God, and joint-heirs with Christ.

Q. 35. What is sanctification?

A. Sanctification is the work of God's free grace,[1] whereby we are renewed in the whole man after the image of God,[2] and are enabled more and more to die unto sin, and live unto righteousness.[3]

[1] 2 *Thess.* 2:13: God hath from the beginning chosen you to salvation through sanctification of the Spirit and belief of the truth.

[2] *Eph.* 4:24: And that ye put on the new man, which after God is created in righteousness and true holiness.

[3] *Rom.* 8:1: There is therefore now no condemnation to them which are in Christ Jesus, who walk not after the flesh, but after the Spirit.

Q. 36. What are the benefits which in this life do

accompany or flow from justification, adoption, and sanctification?

A. The benefits which in this life do accompany or flow from justification, adoption, and sanctification, are, assurance of God's love, peace of conscience, joy in the Holy Ghost,[1] increase of grace,[2] and perseverance therein to the end.[3]

[1] *Rom.* 5:1-2, 5: Therefore being justified by faith, we have peace with God through our Lord Jesus Christ: [2] By whom also we have access by faith into this grace wherein we stand, and rejoice in hope of the glory of God. [5] And hope maketh not ashamed; because the love of God is shed abroad in our hearts by the Holy Ghost which is given unto us.

[2] *Prov.* 4:18: But the path of the just is as the shining light, that shineth more and more unto the perfect day.

[3] 1 *John* 5:13: These things have I written unto you that believe on the name of the Son of God; that ye may know that ye have eternal life.

Q. 37. What benefits do believers receive from Christ at death?

A. The souls of believers are at their death made perfect in holiness,[1] and do immediately pass into glory;[2] and their bodies, being still united to Christ,[3] do rest in their graves[4] till the resurrection.[5]

[1] *Heb.* 12:23: And to God the Judge of all, and to the spirits of just men made perfect.

[2] *Phil.* 1:23: Having a desire to depart, and to be with Christ; which is far better.

[3] 1 *Thess.* 4:14: Them also which sleep in Jesus will God bring with him.

⁴ *Isa.* 57:2: He shall enter into peace: they shall rest in their beds, each one walking in his uprightness.

⁵ *Job* 19:26: And though after my skin worms destroy this body, yet in my flesh shall I see God

Q. 38. What benefits do believers receive from Christ at the resurrection?

A. At the resurrection, believers, being raised up in glory,[1] shall be openly acknowledged and acquitted in the day of judgment,[2] and made perfectly blessed in the full enjoying of God[3] to all eternity.[4]

¹ 1 *Cor.* 15:43: It is sown in dishonour; it is raised in glory.

² *Matt.* 10:32: Whosoever therefore shall confess me before men, him will I confess also before my Father which is in heaven.

³ 1 *John* 3:2: When he shall appear, we shall be like him; for we shall see him as he is.

⁴ 1 *Thess.* 4:17: And so shall we ever be with the Lord.

Q. 39. What is the duty which God requireth of man?

A. The duty which God requireth of man, is obedience to his revealed will.[1]

¹ *Mic.* 6:8: He hath shewed thee, O man, what is good; and what doth the LORD require of thee, but to do justly, and to love mercy, and to walk humbly with thy God?

Q. 40. What did God at first reveal to man for the rule of his obedience?

A. The rule which God at first revealed to man for his obedience, was the moral law.[1]

¹ *Rom.* 2:14-15: For when the Gentiles, which have not the law, do by nature the things contained in the law, these, having not the law, are a law unto themselves ¹⁵ Which shew the work of the law written in their hearts.

Q. 41. Wherein is the moral law summarily comprehended?

A. The moral law is summarily comprehended in the ten commandments.[1]

[1] *Deut.* 10:4: And he wrote on the tables, according to the first writing, the ten commandments, which the LORD spake unto you in the mount out of the midst of the fire in the day of the assembly: and the LORD gave them unto me. *Matt.* 19:17: If thou wilt enter into life, keep the commandments.

Q. 42. What is the sum of the ten commandments?

A. The sum of the ten commandments is, To love the Lord our God with all our heart, with all our soul, with all our strength, and with all our mind; and our neighbour as ourselves.[1]

[1] *Matt.* 22:37-40: Jesus said unto him, Thou shalt love the Lord thy God with all thy heart, and with all thy soul, and with all thy mind. This is the first and great commandment. [39] And the second is like unto it, Thou shalt love thy neighbour as thyself. [40] On these two commandments hang all the law and the prophets.

Q. 43. What is the preface to the ten commandments?

A. The preface to the ten commandments is in these words, *I am the Lord thy God, which have brought thee out of the land of Egypt, out of the house of bondage.*[1]

[1] *Exod.* 20:2.

Q. 44. What doth the preface to the ten commandments teach us?

A. The preface to the ten commandments teacheth us, that because God is the Lord, and our God, and Redeemer, therefore we are bound to keep all his commandments.[1]

[1] *Deut.* 11:1: Therefore thou shalt love the Lord thy God, and keep his charge, and his statutes, and his judgments, and his commandments, alway. *Luke* 1:74-75: That we being delivered out of the hand of our enemies might serve him without fear, [75] In holiness and righteousness before him, all the days of our life.

Q. 45. Which is the first commandment?

A. The first commandment is, *Thou shalt have no other gods before me.*

Q. 46. What is required in the first commandment?

A. The first commandment requireth us to know[1] and acknowledge God to be the only true God, and our God;[2] and to worship and glorify him accordingly.[3]

[1] *1 Chron.* 28:9: And thou, Solomon my son, know thou the God of thy father.
[2] *Deut.* 26:17: Thou hast avouched the Lord this day to be thy God, and to walk in his ways, and to keep his statutes, and his commandments, and his judgments, and to hearken unto his voice.
[3] *Matt.* 4:10: Thou shalt worship the Lord thy God, and him only shalt thou serve.

Q. 47. What is forbidden in the first commandment?

A. The first commandment forbiddeth the denying,[1] or not worshipping and glorifying, the true God as God,[2] and our God;[3] and the giving of that worship and glory to any other, which is due to him alone.[4]

[1] *Psa.* 14:1: The fool hath said in his heart, There is no God.

[2] *Rom.* 1:20-21: So that they are without excuse: [21] Because that, when they knew God, they glorified him not as God.

[3] *Psa.* 81:11: But my people would not hearken to my voice; and Israel would none of me.

[4] *Rom.* 1:25: Who changed the truth of God into a lie, and worshipped and served the creature more than the Creator, who is blessed for ever. Amen.

Q. 48. What are we specially taught by these words *before me* in the first commandment?

A. These words *before me* in the first commandment teach us, That God, who seeth all things, taketh notice of, and is much displeased with, the sin of having any other God.[1]

[1] *Psa.* 44:20-21: If we have forgotten the name of our God, or stretched out our hands to a strange god; [21] Shall not God search this out? for he knoweth the secrets of the heart.

Q. 49. Which is the second commandment?

A. The second commandment is, *Thou shalt not make unto thee any graven image, or any likeness of any thing that is in heaven above, or that is in the earth beneath, or that is in the water under the earth: Thou shalt not bow down thyself to them, nor serve them: for I the* LORD *thy God am a jealous God, visiting the iniquity of the fathers upon the children unto the third and fourth generation of them that hate me; And shewing mercy unto thousands of them that love me, and keep my commandments.*

Q. 50. What is required in the second commandment?

A. The second commandment requireth the receiving, observing,[1] and keeping pure and entire, all such religious worship and ordinances as God hath appointed in his word.[2]

[1] *Deut.* 32:46: And he said unto them, Set your hearts unto all the words which I testify among you this day, which ye shall command your children to observe to do, all the words of this law. *Matt.* 28:20: Teaching them to observe all things whatsoever I have commanded you.
[2] *Deut.* 12:32: What thing soever I command you, observe to do it: thou shalt not add thereto, nor diminish from it.

Q. 51. What is forbidden in the second commandment?

A. The second commandment forbiddeth the worshipping of God by images,[1] or any other way not appointed in his word.[2]

[1] *Deut.* 4:15-16: Take ye therefore good heed unto yourselves; for ye saw no manner of similitude on the day that the LORD spake unto you in Horeb. 16 Lest ye corrupt yourselves, and make you a graven image.
[2] *Col.* 2:18: Let no man beguile you of your reward in a voluntary humility and worshipping of angels, intruding into those things which he hath not seen, vainly puffed up by his fleshly mind.

Q. 52. What are the reasons annexed to the second commandment?

A. The reasons annexed to the second commandment are, God's sovereignty over us,[1] his propriety in us,[2] and the zeal he hath to his own worship.[3]

[1] *Psa.* 95:2-3: Let us come before his presence with thanksgiving,

and make a joyful noise unto him with psalms. [3] For the LORD is a great God, and a great King above all gods.

[2] *Psa.* 45:11: He is thy Lord; and worship thou him.

[3] *Exod.* 34:14: Thou shalt worship no other god: for the LORD, whose name is Jealous, is a jealous God:

Q. 53. Which is the third commandment?

A. The third commandment is, *Thou shalt not take the name of the Lord thy God in vain: for the Lord will not hold him guiltless that taketh his name in vain.*

Q. 54. What is required in the third commandment?

A. The third commandment requireth the holy and reverent use of God's names,[1] titles, attributes,[2] ordinances,[3] word,[4] and works.[5]

[1] *Psa.* 29:2: Give unto the LORD the glory due unto his name.

[2] *Rev.* 15:3-4: Great and marvellous are thy works, Lord God Almighty; just and true are thy ways, thou King of saints. [4] Who shall not fear thee, O Lord, and glorify thy name?

[3] *Eccles.* 5:11: Keep thy foot when thou goest to the house of God, and be more ready to hear, than to give the sacrifice of fools.

[4] *Psa.* 138:2: I will worship toward thy holy temple, and praise thy name for thy lovingkindness and for thy truth: for thou hast magnified thy word above all thy name.

[5] *Job* 36:24: Remember that thou magnify his work, which men behold.

Q. 55. What is forbidden in the third commandment?

A. The third commandment forbiddeth all profaning or abusing of anything whereby God maketh himself known.[1]

[1] *Mal.* 2:2: If ye will not hear, and if ye will not lay it to heart, to

give glory unto my name, saith the LORD of hosts, I will even send a curse upon you.

Q. 56. What is the reason annexed to the third commandment?

A. The reason annexed to the third commandment is, That however the breakers of this commandment may escape punishment from men, yet the Lord our God will not suffer them to escape his righteous judgment.[1]

[1] *Deut.* 28:58-59: If thou wilt not observe to do all the words of this law that are written in this book, that thou mayest fear this glorious and fearful name, THE LORD THY GOD; [59] Then the LORD will make thy plagues wonderful.

Q. 57. Which is the fourth commandment?

A. The fourth commandment is, *Remember the sabbath day to keep it holy. Six days shalt thou labour, and do all thy work: but the seventh day is the sabbath of the Lord thy God: in it thou shalt not do any work, thou, nor thy son, nor thy daughter, thy manservant, nor thy maidservant, nor thy cattle, nor thy stranger that is within thy gates: For in six days the Lord made heaven and earth, the sea, and all that in them is, and rested the seventh day: wherefore the Lord blessed the sabbath day, and hallowed it.*

Q. 58. What is required in the fourth commandment?

A. The fourth commandment requireth the keeping holy to God such set times as he hath appointed in his word; expressly one whole day in seven, to be a holy sabbath to himself.[1]

[1] *Lev.* 19:30: Ye shall keep my sabbaths, and reverence my sanctuary: I am the LORD. *Deut.* 5:12: Keep the sabbath day to sanctify it, as the LORD thy God hath commanded thee.

Q. 59. Which day of the seven hath God appointed to be the weekly sabbath?

A. From the beginning of the world to the resurrection of Christ, God appointed the seventh day of the week to be the weekly sabbath;[1] and the first day of the week ever since, to continue to the end of the world, which is the Christian sabbath.[2]

[1] *Gen.* 2:3: And God blessed the seventh day, and sanctified it: because that in it he had rested from all his work which God created and made.

[2] *Acts* 20:7: And upon the first day of the week, when the disciples came together to break bread, Paul preached unto them. *Rev.* 1:10: I was in the Spirit on the Lord's day.

Q. 60. How is the sabbath to be sanctified?

A. The sabbath is to be sanctified by a holy resting all that day, even from such worldly employments and recreations as are lawful on other days;[1] and spending the whole time in the public and private exercises of God's worship,[2] except so much as is to be taken up in the works of necessity and mercy.[3]

[1] *Lev.* 23:3: Six days shall work be done: but the seventh day is the sabbath of rest, an holy convocation; ye shall do no work therein.

[2] *Psa.* 92:1-2: (A Psalm or Song for the sabbath day.) It is a good thing

to give thanks unto the LORD, and to sing praises unto thy name, O most High: [2] To shew forth thy lovingkindness in the morning, and thy faithfulness every night.

[3] *Matt.* 12:11-12: And he said unto them, What man shall there be among you, that shall have one sheep, and if it fall into a pit on the sabbath day, will he not lay hold on it, and lift it out? [12] How much then is a man better than a sheep? Wherefore it is lawful to do well on the sabbath days.

Q. 61. What is forbidden in the fourth commandment?

A. The fourth commandment forbiddeth the omission, or careless performance, of the duties required,[1] and the profaning the day by idleness, or doing that which is in itself sinful,[2] or by unnecessary thoughts, words, or works, about our worldly employments or recreations.[3]

[1] *Mal.* 1:13: Ye said also, Behold, what a weariness is it! and ye have snuffed at it, saith the LORD of hosts; and ye brought that which was torn, and the lame, and the sick; thus ye brought an offering: should I accept this of your hand? saith the LORD.

[2] *Ezek.* 23:38: They have defiled my sanctuary in the same day, and have profaned my sabbaths.

[3] *Isa.* 58:13: If thou turn away thy foot from the sabbath, from doing thy pleasure on my holy day; and call the sabbath a delight, the holy of the LORD, honourable; and shalt honour him, not doing thine own ways, nor finding thine own pleasure, nor speaking thine own words.

Q. 62. What are the reasons annexed to the fourth commandment?

A. The reasons annexed to the fourth commandment are, God's allowing us six days of the week for our own employments,[1] his challenging a special propriety in the seventh,[2] his own example,[3] and his blessing the sabbath day.[4]

[1] *Exod.* 31:15-16: Six days may work be done; but in the seventh is the sabbath of rest. [16] Wherefore the children of Israel shall keep the sabbath.

[2] *Lev.* 23:3: Ye shall do no work therein: it is the sabbath of the LORD in all your dwellings.

[3] *Exod.* 31:17: It is a sign between me and the children of Israel for ever: for in six days the LORD made heaven and earth, and on the seventh day he rested, and was refreshed.

[4] *Gen.* 2:3: And God blessed the seventh day, and sanctified it.

Q. 63. Which is the fifth commandment?

A. The fifth commandment is, *Honour thy father and thy mother: that thy days may be long upon the land which the Lord thy God giveth thee.*

Q. 64. What is required in the fifth commandment?

A. The fifth commandment requireth the preserving the honour, and performing the duties, belonging to every-one in their several places and relations, as superiors,[1] inferiors,[2] or equals.[3]

[1] *Eph.* 5:21-22: Submitting yourselves one to another in the fear of God. [22] Wives, submit yourselves unto your own husbands, as unto the Lord. *Eph.* 6:1, 5: Children, obey your parents in the Lord. [5] Servants, be obedient to them that are your masters according to the flesh. *Rom.* 13:1: Let every soul be subject unto the higher powers.

[2] *Eph.* 6:9: And, ye masters, do the same things unto them, forbearing threatening: knowing that your Master also is in heaven.

[3] *Rom.* 12:10: Be kindly affectioned one to another with brotherly love; in honour preferring one another.

Q. 65. What is forbidden in the fifth commandment?

A. The fifth commandment forbiddeth the neglecting of, or doing anything against, the honour and duty which belongeth to everyone in their several places and relations.[1]

[1] *Rom.* 13:7-8: Render therefore to all their dues: tribute to whom tribute is due; custom to whom custom; fear to whom fear; honour to whom honour. [8] Owe no man any thing, but to love one another.

Q. 66. What is the reason annexed to the fifth commandment?

A. The reason annexed to the fifth commandment is, a promise of long life and prosperity (as far as it shall serve for God's glory and their own good) to all such as keep this commandment.[1]

[1] *Eph.* 6:2-3: Honour thy father and mother; (which is the first commandment with promise;) [3] That it may be well with thee, and thou mayest live long on the earth.

Q. 67. Which is the sixth commandment?

A. The sixth commandment is, *Thou shalt not kill.*

Q. 68. What is required in the sixth commandment?

A. The sixth commandment requireth all lawful endeavours to preserve our own life,[1] and the life of others.[2]

[1] *Eph.* 5:28: So ought men to love their wives as their own bodies. He that loveth his wife loveth himself.
[2] *Psa.* 82:3-4: Defend the poor and fatherless: do justice to the afflicted and needy. [4] Deliver the poor and needy. *Job* 29:13: The blessing of him that was ready to perish came upon me.

Q. 69. What is forbidden in the sixth commandment?

A. The sixth commandment forbiddeth the taking away of our own life,[1] or the life of our neighbour unjustly,[2] or whatsoever tendeth thereunto.[3]

[1] *Acts* 16:28: But Paul cried with a loud voice, saying, Do thyself no harm.

[2] *Gen.* 9:6: Whoso sheddeth man's blood, by man shall his blood be shed.

[3] *Prov.* 24:11-12: If thou forbear to deliver them that are drawn unto death, and those that are ready to be slain; [12] If thou sayest, Behold, we knew it not; doth not he that pondereth the heart consider it?

Q. 70. Which is the seventh commandment?

A. The seventh commandment is, *Thou shalt not commit adultery.*

Q. 71. What is required in the seventh commandment?

A. The seventh commandment requireth the preservation of our own[1] and our neighbour's chastity,[2] in heart,[3] speech,[4] and behaviour.[5]

[1] 1 *Thess.* 4:4: That every one of you should know how to possess his vessel in sanctification and honour.

[2] *Eph.* 5:11-12: And have no fellowship with the unfruitful works of darkness, but rather reprove them. [12] For it is a shame even to speak of those things which are done of them in secret.

[3] 2 *Tim.* 2:22: Flee also youthful lusts: but follow righteousness, faith, charity, peace.

[4] *Col.* 4:6: Let your speech be alway with grace, seasoned with salt.

[5] 1 *Pet.* 3:2: While they behold your chaste conversation coupled with fear.

Q. 72. What is forbidden in the seventh commandment?

A. The seventh commandment forbiddeth all unchaste thoughts,[1] words,[2] and actions.[3]

[1] *Matt.* 5:28: Whosoever looketh on a woman to lust after her hath committed adultery with her already in his heart.
[2] *Eph.* 5:4: Neither filthiness, nor foolish talking, nor jesting, which are not convenient.
[3] *Eph.* 5:3: Fornication, and all uncleanness, or covetousness, let it not be once named among you, as becometh saints.

Q. 73. Which is the eighth commandment?

A. The eighth commandment is, *Thou shalt not steal.*

Q. 74. What is required in the eighth commandment?

A. The eighth commandment requireth the lawful procuring and furthering the wealth and outward estate of ourselves[1] and others.[2]

[1] *Rom.* 12:17: Provide things honest in the sight of all men. *Prov.* 27:23: Be thou diligent to know the state of thy flocks, and look well to thy herds.
[2] *Lev.* 25:35: And if thy brother be waxen poor, and fallen in decay with thee; then thou shalt relieve him. *Phil.* 2:4: Look not every man on his own things, but every man also on the things of others.

Q. 75. What is forbidden in the eighth commandment?

A. The eighth commandment forbiddeth whatsoever doth, or may, unjustly hinder our own,[1] or our neighbour's wealth or outward estate.[2]

¹ *1 Tim.* 5:8: If any provide not for his own, and specially for those of his own house, he hath denied the faith, and is worse than an infidel.
² *Prov.* 28:19: He that followeth after vain persons shall have poverty enough. *Prov.* 21:6: The getting of treasures by a lying tongue is a vanity tossed to and fro of them that seek death. *Job* 20:19-20: Because he hath oppressed and hath forsaken the poor; because he hath violently taken away an house which he builded not; ²⁰ Surely he shall not feel quietness in his belly, he shall not save of that which he desired.

Q. 76. Which is the ninth commandment?

A. The ninth commandment is, *Thou shalt not bear false witness against thy neighbour.*

Q. 77. What is required in the ninth commandment?

A. The ninth commandment requireth the maintaining and promoting of truth between man and man,¹ and of our own² and our neighbour's good name.³ especially in witness-bearing.⁴

¹ *Zech.* 8:16: Speak ye every man the truth to his neighbour.
² *1 Pet.* 3:16: Having a good conscience; that, whereas they speak evil of you, as of evildoers, they may be ashamed that falsely accuse your good conversation in Christ. *Acts* 25:10: Then said Paul, I stand at Caesar's judgment seat, where I ought to be judged: to the Jews have I done no wrong.
³ *3 John* 12: Demetrius hath good report of all men, and of the truth itself: yea, and we also bear record.
⁴ *Prov.* 14:5, 25: A faithful witness will not lie: but a false witness will utter lies. ²⁵ A true witness delivereth souls: but a deceitful witness speaketh lies.

Q. 78. What is forbidden in the ninth commandment?

A. The ninth commandment forbiddeth whatsoever is prejudicial to truth,[1] or injurious to our own,[2] or our neighbour's, good name.[3]

[1] *Rom.* 3:13: With their tongues they have used deceit.
[2] *Job* 27:5: God forbid that I should justify you: till I die I will not remove mine integrity from me.
[3] *Psa.* 15:3: He that backbiteth not with his tongue, nor doeth evil to his neighbour, nor taketh up a reproach against his neighbour.

Q. 79. Which is the tenth commandment?

A. The tenth commandment is, *Thou shalt not covet thy neighbour's house, thou shalt not covet thy neighbour's wife, nor his manservant, nor his maidservant, nor his ox, nor his ass, nor anything that is thy neighbour's.*

Q. 80. What is required in the tenth commandment?

A. The tenth commandment requireth full contentment with our own condition,[1] with a right and charitable frame of spirit toward our neighbour, and all that is his.[2]

[1] *Heb.* 13:5: Let your conversation be without covetousness; and be content with such things as ye have.
[2] *Rom.* 12:15: Rejoice with them that do rejoice, and weep with them that weep. 1 *Cor.* 13:4-6: Charity suffereth long, and is kind; charity envieth not; charity vaunteth not itself, is not puffed up, [5] Doth not behave itself unseemly, seeketh not her own, is not easily provoked, thinketh no evil; [6] Rejoiceth not in iniquity, but rejoiceth in the truth.

Q. 81. What is forbidden in the tenth commandment?

A. The tenth commandment forbiddeth all discontentment with our own estate,[1] envying or grieving at the good of our neighbour,[2] and all inordinate motions and affections to anything that is his.[3]

[1] *1 Cor.* 10:10: Neither murmur ye, as some of them also murmured, and were destroyed of the destroyer.
[2] *Gal.* 5:26: Let us not be desirous of vain glory, provoking one another, envying one another.
[3] *Col.* 3:5: Mortify therefore your members which are upon the earth; fornication, uncleanness, inordinate affection, evil concupiscence, and covetousness, which is idolatry.

Q. 82. Is any man able perfectly to keep the commandments of God?

A. No mere man, since the fall, is able in this life perfectly to keep the commandments of God,[1] but doth daily break them in thought,[2] word,[3] and deed.[4]

[1] *Eccles.* 7:20: For there is not a just man upon earth, that doeth good, and sinneth not.
[2] *Gen.* 8:21: For the imagination of man's heart is evil from his youth.
[3] *James* 3:8: But the tongue can no man tame; it is an unruly evil, full of deadly poison.
[4] *James* 3:2: In many things we offend all.

Q. 83. Are all transgressions of the law equally heinous?

A. Some sins in themselves, and by reason of several aggravations, are more heinous in the sight of God than others.[1]

[1] *John* 19:11: He that delivered me unto thee hath the greater sin.

Q. 84. What doth every sin deserve?

A. Every sin deserveth God's wrath and curse, both in this life, and that which is to come.[1]

[1] *Gal.* 3:10: Cursed is every one that continueth not in all things which are written in the book of the law to do them. *Matt.* 25:41: Then shall he say also unto them on the left hand, Depart from me, ye cursed, into everlasting fire, prepared for the devil and his angels.

Q. 85. What doth God require of us, that we may escape his wrath and curse due to us for sin?

A. To escape the wrath and curse of God due to us for sin, God requireth of us faith in Jesus Christ, repentance unto life,[1] with the diligent use of all the outward means whereby Christ communicateth to us the benefits of redemption.[2]

[1] *Acts* 20:21: Testifying both to the Jews, and also to the Greeks, repentance toward God, and faith toward our Lord Jesus Christ.
[2] *Prov.* 2:1-5 My son, if thou wilt receive my words, and hide my commandments with thee; [2] So that thou incline thine ear unto wisdom, and apply thine heart to understanding; [3] Yea, if thou criest after knowledge, and liftest up thy voice for understanding; [4] If thou seekest her as silver, and searchest for her as for hid treasures; [5] Then shalt thou understand the fear of the LORD, and find the knowledge of God.

Q. 86. What is faith in Jesus Christ?

A. Faith in Jesus Christ is a saving grace,[1] whereby we receive[2] and rest upon him alone for salvation,[3] as he is offered to us in the gospel.[4]

[1] *Heb.* 10:39: But we are not of them who draw back unto perdition; but of them that believe to the saving of the soul.
[2] *John* 1:12: But as many as received him, to them gave he power to become the sons of God, even to them that believe on his name:
[3] *Phil.* 3:9: And be found in him, not having mine own righteousness, which is of the law, but that which is through the faith of Christ, the righteousness which is of God by faith.

4 *Isa.* 33:22: For the LORD is our judge, the LORD is our lawgiver, the LORD is our king; he will save us.

Q. 87. What is repentance unto life?

A. Repentance unto life is a saving grace,[1] whereby a sinner, out of a true sense of his sin,[2] and apprehension of the mercy of God in Christ,[3] doth, with grief and hatred of his sin, turn from it unto God,[4] with full purpose of, and endeavour after, new obedience.[5]

[1] *Acts* 11:18: Then hath God also to the Gentiles granted repentance unto life.

[2] *Acts* 2:37: When they heard this, they were pricked in their heart, and said unto Peter and to the rest of the apostles, Men and brethren, what shall we do?

[3] *Joel* 2:13: Rend your heart, and not your garments, and turn unto the LORD your God: for he is gracious and merciful, slow to anger, and of great kindness, and repenteth him of the evil.

[4] *Jer.* 31:18-19: Turn thou me, and I shall be turned; for thou art the LORD my God. [19] Surely after that I was turned, I repented; and after that I was instructed, I smote upon my thigh: I was ashamed, yea, even confounded, because I did bear the reproach of my youth.

[5] *Psa.* 119:59: I thought on my ways, and turned my feet unto thy testimonies.

Q. 88. What are the outward and ordinary means whereby Christ communicateth to us the benefits of redemption?

A. The outward and ordinary means whereby Christ communicateth to us the benefits of redemption are, his ordinances, especially the word, sacraments, and prayer;[1] all which are made effectual to the elect for salvation.

[1] *Acts* 2:41-42: Then they that gladly received his word were baptized:

[37]

and the same day there were added unto them about three thousand souls. [42] And they continued stedfastly in the apostles' doctrine and fellowship, and in breaking of bread, and in prayers.

Q. 89. How is the word made effectual to salvation?

A. The Spirit of God maketh the reading, but especially the preaching, of the word, an effectual means of convincing and converting sinners,[1] and of building them up in holiness and comfort,[2] through faith, unto salvation.[3]

[1] *Psa.* 19:7: The law of the LORD is perfect, converting the soul.
[2] 1 *Thess.* 1:6: And ye became followers of us, and of the Lord, having received the word in much affliction, with joy of the Holy Ghost.
[3] *Rom.* 1:16: For I am not ashamed of the gospel of Christ: for it is the power of God unto salvation to every one that believeth.

Q. 90. How is the word to be read and heard, that it may become effectual to salvation?

A. That the word may become effectual to salvation, we must attend thereunto with diligence,[1] preparation,[2] and prayer;[3] receive it with faith[4] and love,[5] lay it up in our hearts,[6] and practice it in our lives.[7]

[1] *Prov.* 8:34: Blessed is the man that heareth me, watching daily at my gates, waiting at the posts of my doors.
[2] 1 *Pet.* 2:1-2: Wherefore laying aside all malice, and all guile, and hypocrisies, and envies, and all evil speakings, [2] As newborn babes, desire the sincere milk of the word, that ye may grow thereby.
[3] *Psa.* 119:18: Open thou mine eyes, that I may behold wondrous things out of thy law.
[4] *Heb.* 4:2: The word preached did not profit them, not being mixed with faith in them that heard it.
[5] 2 *Thess.* 2:10: They received not the love of the truth, that they might be saved.

[6] *Psa.* 119:11: Thy word have I hid in mine heart, that I might not sin against thee.

[7] *James* 1:25: But whoso looketh into the perfect law of liberty, and continueth therein, he being not a forgetful hearer, but a doer of the work, this man shall be blessed in his deed.

Q. 91. How do the sacraments become effectual means of salvation?

A. The sacraments become effectual means of salvation, not from any virtue in them, or in him that doth administer them;[1] but only by the blessing of Christ, and the working of his Spirit in them that by faith receive them.[2]

[1] 1 *Cor.* 3:7: So then neither is he that planteth any thing, neither he that watereth; but God that giveth the increase.

[2] 1 *Pet.* 3:21: The like figure whereunto even baptism doth also now save us (not the putting away of the filth of the flesh, but the answer of a good conscience toward God,) by the resurrection of Jesus Christ.

Q. 92. What is a sacrament?

A. A sacrament is an holy ordinance instituted by Christ;[1] wherein, by sensible signs, Christ, and the benefits of the new covenant, are represented, sealed, and applied to believers.[2]

[1] *Gen.* 17:10: This is my covenant, which ye shall keep, between me and you and thy seed after thee; Every man child among you shall be circumcised.

[2] *Rom.* 4:11: And he received the sign of circumcision, a seal of the righteousness of the faith which he had yet being uncircumcised.

Q. 93. Which are the sacraments of the New Testament?

A. The sacraments of the New Testament are, baptism,[1] and the Lord's Supper.[2]

[1] *Mark* 16:16: He that believeth and is baptized shall be saved.
[2] 1 *Cor.* 11:23: For I have received of the Lord that which also I delivered unto you, That the Lord Jesus the same night in which he was betrayed took bread.

Q. 94. What is baptism?

A. Baptism is a sacrament, wherein the washing with water in the name of the Father, and of the Son, and of the Holy Ghost,[1] doth signify and seal our ingrafting into Christ, and partaking of the benefits of the covenant of grace,[2] and our engagement to be the Lord's.[3]

[1] *Matt.* 28:19: Go ye therefore, and teach all nations, baptizing them in the name of the Father, and of the Son, and of the Holy Ghost.
[2] *Rom.* 6:3: Know ye not, that so many of us as were baptized into Jesus Christ were baptized into his death?
[3] *Rom.* 6:4: Therefore we are buried with him by baptism into death: that like as Christ was raised up from the dead by the glory of the Father, even so we also should walk in newness of life.

Q. 95. To whom is Baptism to be administered?

A. Baptism is not to be administered to any that are out of the visible church, till they profess their faith in Christ, and obedience to him;[1] but the infants of such as are members of the visible church are to be baptized.[2]

[1] *Acts* 2:41: Then they that gladly received his word were baptized.
[2] *Gen.* 17:7, 10: And I will establish my covenant between me and thee and thy seed after thee in their generations for an everlasting covenant, to be a God unto thee, and to thy seed after thee. [10] This

is my covenant, which ye shall keep, between me and you and thy seed after thee; Every man child among you shall be circumcised. *Acts* 2:38: Then Peter said unto them, Repent, and be baptized every one of you in the name of Jesus Christ for the remission of sins, and ye shall receive the gift of the Holy Ghost. [39] For the promise is unto you, and to your children, and to all that are afar off, even as many as the Lord our God shall call.

Q. 96. What is the Lord's Supper?

A. The Lord's Supper is a sacrament, wherein, by giving and receiving bread and wine, according to Christ's appointment, his death is showed forth;[1] and the worthy receivers are, not after a corporal and carnal manner, but by faith, made partakers of his body and blood, with all his benefits, to their spiritual nourishment, and growth in grace.[2]

[1] *Luke* 22:19-20: And he took bread, and gave thanks, and brake it, and gave unto them, saying, This is my body which is given for you: this do in remembrance of me. [20] Likewise also the cup after supper, saying, This cup is the new testament in my blood, which is shed for you.
[2] 1 *Cor.* 10:16: The cup of blessing which we bless, is it not the communion of the blood of Christ? The bread which we break, is it not the communion of the body of Christ?

Q. 97. What is required to the worthy receiving of the Lord's Supper?

A. It is required of them that would worthily partake of the Lord's Supper, that they examine themselves of their knowledge to discern the Lord's body,[1] of their faith to feed upon him,[2] of their repentance,[3] love,[4] and new obedience;[5] lest, coming unworthily, they eat and drink judgment to themselves.[6]

[1] *1 Cor.* 11:28-29: But let a man examine himself, and so let him eat of that bread, and drink of that cup. [29] For he that eateth and drinketh unworthily, eateth and drinketh damnation to himself, not discerning the Lord's body.

[2] *2 Cor.* 13:5: Examine yourselves, whether ye be in the faith.

[3] *1 Cor.* 11:31: For if we would judge ourselves, we should not be judged.

[4] *1 Cor.* 11:18, 20: When ye come together in the church, I hear that there be divisions among you. [20] When ye come together therefore into one place, this is not to eat the Lord's supper.

[5] *1 Cor.* 5:8: Therefore let us keep the feast, not with old leaven, neither with the leaven of malice and wickedness; but with the unleavened bread of sincerity and truth.

[6] *1 Cor.* 11:27: Wherefore whosoever shall eat this bread, and drink this cup of the Lord, unworthily, shall be guilty of the body and blood of the Lord.

Q. 98. What is prayer?

A. Prayer is an offering up of our desires unto God,[1] for things agreeable to his will,[2] in the name of Christ,[3] with confession of our sins,[4] and thankful acknowledgment of his mercies.[5]

[1] *Psa.* 62:8: Trust in him at all times; ye people, pour out your heart before him: God is a refuge for us.

[2] *Rom.* 8:27: And he that searcheth the hearts knoweth what is the mind of the Spirit, because he maketh intercession for the saints according to the will of God.

[3] *John* 16:23: Whatsoever ye shall ask the Father in my name, he will give it you.

[4] *Dan.* 9:4: And I prayed unto the LORD my God, and made my confession.

[5] *Phil.* 4:6: Be careful for nothing; but in every thing by prayer and supplication with thanksgiving let your requests be made known unto God.

Q. 99. What rule hath God given for our direction in prayer?

A. The whole Word of God is of use to direct us in prayer;[1] but the special rule of direction is that form of prayer which Christ taught his disciples, commonly called *The Lord's Prayer.*[2]

[1] *1 John* 5:14: And this is the confidence that we have in him, that, if we ask any thing according to his will, he heareth us.
[2] *Matt.* 6:9: After this manner therefore pray ye: Our Father which art in heaven, Hallowed be thy name, &c.

Q. 100. What doth the preface of the Lord's Prayer teach us?

A. The preface of the Lord's Prayer, (which is, *Our Father which art in heaven,*) teacheth us to draw near to God with all holy reverence and confidence,[1] as children to a father;[2] able and ready to help us;[3] and that we should pray with and for others.[4]

[1] *Isa.* 64:9: Be not wroth very sore, O LORD, neither remember iniquity for ever: behold, see, we beseech thee, we are all thy people.
[2] *Luke* 11:13: If ye then, being evil, know how to give good gifts unto your children: how much more shall your heavenly Father give the Holy Spirit to them that ask him?
[3] *Rom.* 8:15: For ye have not received the spirit of bondage again to fear; but ye have received the Spirit of adoption, whereby we cry, Abba, Father.
[4] *Eph.* 6:18: Praying always with all prayer and supplication in the Spirit, and watching thereunto with all perseverance and supplication for all saints.

Q. 101. What do we pray for in the first petition?

A. In the first petition, (which is, *Hallowed be thy name,*) we pray, That God would enable us, and others, to glorify him in all that whereby he maketh himself known;[1] and that he would dispose all things to his own glory.[2]

[1] *Psa.* 67:1-3: God be merciful unto us, and bless us; and cause his face to shine upon us; [2] That thy way may be known upon earth, thy saving health among all nations. [3] Let the people praise thee, O God; let all the people praise thee.

[2] *Rom.* 11:36: For of him, and through him, and to him, are all things: to whom be glory for ever. Amen.

Q. 102. What do we pray for in the second petition?

A. In the second petition, (which is, *Thy kingdom come,*) we pray, That Satan's kingdom may be destroyed;[1] and that the kingdom of grace may be advanced,[2] ourselves and others brought into it, and kept in it;[3] and that the kingdom of glory may be hastened.[4]

[1] *Psa.* 68:1: Let God arise, let his enemies be scattered: let them also that hate him flee before him.

[2] *Psa.* 51:18: Do good in thy good pleasure unto Zion: build thou the walls of Jerusalem.

[3] 2 *Thess.* 3:1: Finally, brethren, pray for us, that the word of the Lord may have free course, and be glorified, even as it is with you. *Rom.* 10:1: Brethren, my heart's desire and prayer to God for Israel is, that they might be saved.

[4] *Rev.* 22:20: He which testifieth these things saith, Surely I come quickly. Amen. Even so, come, Lord Jesus.

Q. 103. What do we pray for in the third petition?

A. In the third petition, (which is, *Thy will be done in earth, as it is in heaven,*) we pray, That God, by his grace, would make us able and willing to know, obey,[1] and submit to his will in all things,[2] as the angels do in heaven.[3]

[1] *Psa.* 119:34-36: Give me understanding, and I shall keep thy law; yea, I shall observe it with my whole heart. [35] Make me to go in the path of thy commandments; for therein do I delight. [36] Incline my heart unto thy testimonies, and not to covetousness.

[2] *Acts* 21:14: And when he would not be persuaded, we ceased, saying, The will of the Lord be done.

[3] *Psa.* 103:20, 22: Bless the LORD, ye his angels, that excel in strength, that do his commandments, hearkening unto the voice of his word. [22] Bless the LORD, all his works in all places of his dominion: bless the LORD, O my soul.

Q. 104. What do we pray for in the fourth petition?

A. In the fourth petition, which is, (*Give us this day our daily bread,*) we pray, That of God's free gift we may receive a competent portion of the good things of this life,[1] and enjoy his blessing with them.[2]

[1] *Prov.* 30:8: Remove far from me vanity and lies: give me neither poverty nor riches; feed me with food convenient for me.

[2] *Psa.* 90:17: And let the beauty of the LORD our God be upon us: and establish thou the work of our hands upon us; yea, the work of our hands establish thou it.

Q. 105. What do we pray for in the fifth petition?

A. In the fifth petition, (which is, *And forgive us our debts, as we forgive our debtors,*) we pray, That God, for Christ's sake, would freely pardon all our sins;[1] which we are the rather encouraged to ask, because by his grace we are enabled from the heart to forgive others.[2]

[1] *Psa.* 51:1: Have mercy upon me, O God, according to thy loving-kindness: according unto the multitude of thy tender mercies blot out my transgressions.

[2] *Matt.* 6:14: For if ye forgive men their trespasses, your heavenly Father will also forgive you.

Q. 106. What do we pray for in the sixth petition?

A. In the sixth petition, (which is, *And lead us not into temptation, but deliver us from evil,*) we pray, That God would either keep us from being tempted to sin,[1] or support and deliver us when we are tempted.[2]

[1] *Matt.* 26:41: Watch and pray, that ye enter not into temptation. *Psa.* 19:13: Keep back thy servant also from presumptuous sins; let them not have dominion over me.

[2] *Psa.* 51:10,12: Create in me a clean heart, O God; and renew a right spirit within me. [12] Restore unto me the joy of thy salvation; and uphold me with thy free spirit.

Q. 107. What doth the conclusion of the Lord's Prayer teach us?

A. The conclusion of the Lord's Prayer, (which is, *For thine is the kingdom, and the power, and the glory, forever. Amen,*) teacheth us to take our encouragement in prayer from God only,[1] and in our prayers to praise him, ascribing kingdom, power, and glory to him.[2] And, in testimony of our desire, and assurance to be heard, we say, Amen.[3]

[1] *Dan.* 9:18-19: We do not present our supplications before thee for our righteousnesses, but for thy great mercies. [19] O Lord, hear; O Lord, forgive; O Lord, hearken and do; defer not, for thine own sake, O my God.

² 1 *Chron.* 29:11, 13: Thine, O LORD, is the greatness, and the power, and the glory, and the victory, and the majesty: for all that is in the heaven and in the earth is thine; thine is the kingdom, O LORD, and thou art exalted as head above all. ¹³ Now therefore, our God, we thank thee, and praise thy glorious name.

³ *Rev.* 22:20: Amen. Even so, come, Lord Jesus.

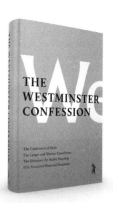

The Westminster Confession

Containing: The Confession of Faith, The Larger and Shorter Catechisms, The Directory for Public Worship, with associated historical documents

'Language fails to assess the blessing that God in his sovereign providence and grace bestowed upon his church through these statements of the Christian faith.' —*Professor John Murray*

ISBN 978 1 84871 768 8 | clothbound | 688pp.